To:

_____

From:

_____

Date:

_____

Miracle Moments for Women

© 2010 Christian Art Gifts, RSA
Christian Art Gifts Inc., IL, USA

Designed by Christian Art Gifts

Images used under license from Shutterstock.com

Scripture quotations marked NLT are taken from the *Holy Bible*, New Living Translation, second edition, copyright © 1996, 2004. Used by permission of Tyndale House Publishers, Inc., Carol Stream, Illinois 60188. All rights reserved.

Scripture quotations are taken from *The Message*. Copyright © by Eugene H. Peterson, 1993, 1994, 1995, 1996, 2000, 2001, 2002. Used by permission of NavPress Publishing Group.

Scripture quotations are taken from the *Holy Bible*, New Century Version®. Copyright © 2005 by Thomas Nelson, Inc. Used by permission. All rights reserved.

Scripture quotations are taken from the *Holy Bible*, New International Version® NIV®. Copyright © 1973, 1978, 1984 by International Bible Society. Used by permission of Zondervan Publishing House. All rights reserved.

Scripture quotations are taken from the *Holy Bible*, New King James Version, copyright © 1982 by Thomas Nelson, Inc., Publishers. Used by permission.

Printed in China

ISBN 978-1-77036-436-3

10 11 12 13 14 15 16 17 18 19 – 11 10 9 8 7 6 5 4 3 2

MIRACLE
MOMENTS
for WOMEN

KAREN MOORE

Contents

This book is dedicated to my sisters – Donna Ryan, Sharon Mirabito, and Stephanie Young, three women who have been the miracle in my life always. God knew what He was doing when He gave me each of you!

Love,

Karen

Introduction

I never had any difficulty believing in miracles, since I experienced the miracle of a change in my own heart. – St. Augustine

Miracle Moments happen all the time. Some of us see them everywhere we turn. Some never seem to notice them at all. Others might think God is no longer in the miracle business. The truth rests in what we believe and what we are careful to observe.

Let the pages of this book remind you of miracles that happened to our biblical ancestors and help you see why they are still relevant today. We'll look at miraculous answers to prayer that will help strengthen our faith and make us into continual prayer warriors. We'll read some amazing stories of family and friendship miracles and, finally, we'll look at those tender miracles that happen all the time in the lives of women everywhere.

As you read about these Miracle Moments, may your heart be opened to those that God has waiting for you. May you see Him in fresh ways as He helps you discover more of His presence in your everyday life.

May you be blessed, dear readers, with a lifetime of love and precious Miracle Moments all your own ...

Through the miracle of His love,

Karen Moore

Section One

Miracle Moments from the Bible

Let's look at each of these stories from the Old and New Testaments with an eye for the miracle itself, and an opportunity for how it might help strengthen our faith as women today.

Though the Bible offers many such stories, only a few are related here. May we discover a fresh viewpoint of what God would have us know of His amazing miracle-working power and grace.

● ● ●

> The first miracle for
> any of us is the one
> that asks us to believe ...
> With God all things
> are possible!

The account in Mark 9:22 is a powerful one because it addresses the concerns many of us might have about any miracles. It looks at our faith and it looks at our doubt and it comes to one conclusion.

Here's the biblical account for us to consider:

THE BIBLICAL ACCOUNT

"When Jesus, Peter, James, and John came back to the other followers, they saw a great crowd around them and the teachers of the law arguing with them. But as soon as the crowd saw Jesus, the people were surprised and ran to welcome Him. Jesus asked, 'What are you arguing about?'

A man answered, 'Teacher, I brought my son to You. He has an evil spirit in him that stops him from talking. When the spirit attacks him, it throws him on the ground. Then my son foams at the mouth, grinds his teeth, and becomes very stiff. I asked Your followers to force the evil spirit out, but they couldn't.'

Jesus answered, 'You people have no faith. How long must I stay with you? How long must I put up with you? Bring the boy to Me.' So the followers brought him to Jesus.

As soon as the evil spirit saw Jesus, it made the boy lose control of himself, and he fell down and rolled on the ground, foaming at the mouth. Jesus asked the boy's father, 'How long has this been happening?' The father answered, 'Since he was very young. The spirit often throws him into a fire or into water to kill him. If You can do anything for him, please have pity on us and help us.'

Jesus said to the father, 'You said, 'If you can!'

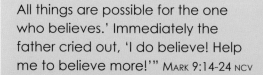

All things are possible for the one who believes.' Immediately the father cried out, 'I do believe! Help me to believe more!'" MARK 9:14-24 NCV

10

Can Grandmothers Have Babies?
Take a Look at Sarah's Son!

THE BIBLICAL ACCOUNT

"'Where is Sarah, your wife?' the visitors asked. 'She's inside the tent,' Abraham replied. Then one of them said, 'I will return to you about this time next year, and your wife, Sarah, will have a son!'

Sarah was listening to this conversation from the tent. Abraham and Sarah were both very old by this time, and Sarah was long past the age of having children. So she laughed silently to herself and said, 'How could a worn-out woman like me enjoy such pleasure, especially when my master – my husband – is also so old?'

Then the LORD said to Abraham, 'Why did Sarah laugh? Why did she say, 'Can an old woman like me have a baby?' Is anything too hard for the LORD? I will return about this time next year, and Sarah will have a son.'

Sarah was afraid, so she denied it, saying, 'I didn't laugh.' But the LORD said, 'No, you did laugh.'"

GENESIS 18:9-15 NLT

Embracing the Miracle Moment ...

Have you ever stood so long on the promises of God without getting the desires of your heart that you finally just chose to believe it was not meant to be?

Did you ever pray so hard, but then watch your circumstances get so out of your control that you just gave up?

Maybe you can identify with Sarah more than you thought as you approach life's practical considerations with your intellect. What could seem more unlikely than a woman whose body had long ago ceased to provide a nurturing womb for having a baby? Grandmothers just assume that child-bearing years are beyond them. Isn't that true for all of us?

Sarah had hoped and prayed and believed that she would have a child ... sometime. She was certain that the God who directed the steps of her husband, Abraham, and watched over them through incredible odds, would bless her with a child.

She believed, she hoped, she prayed. Nothing happened. Her body changed, her opportunity seemed to dry up, so finally she did the only thing she could – she gave up hope. She accepted that it just wasn't meant to be.

What can we learn from Sarah's story? We can either wonder what took God so long, or we can see it in all its glory ... the God of the universe is saying to Sarah and to us, "Nothing is too hard for Me. I can change the circumstances. I made your body and I can return and renew it at any time."

In this case, He did not even ask Sarah to believe Him.

He simply told her not to deny that she laughed about it. Whether she believed it or not, He promised to return and to do what He said He would.

Sarah had the same beliefs that some of us have. She thought she was smart enough to know that having a baby was impossible. She thought her time had run out. She thought there was nothing to be done and that she would simply die an old, barren, forgotten woman. She thought wrong!

Now let's look at the outcome:

"GOD visited Sarah exactly as He said He would; GOD did to Sarah what He promised: Sarah became pregnant and gave Abraham a son in his old age, and at the very time GOD had set. Abraham named him Isaac. When his son was eight days old, Abraham circumcised him just as GOD had commanded.

Abraham was a hundred years old when his son Isaac was born. Sarah said, 'God has blessed me with laughter and all who get the news will laugh with me!'

She also said, 'Whoever would have suggested to Abraham that Sarah would one day nurse a baby! Yet here I am! I've given the old man a son!' The baby grew and was weaned. Abraham threw a big party on the day Isaac was weaned." GENESIS 21:1-8 THE MESSAGE

One Miracle Moment

There's probably not a mom anywhere who wouldn't call having a baby a miracle. Isaac was a miracle baby. His name means "God is laughing now." Even though both Abraham and Sarah had laughed at the idea of having a son in their advanced age, God had prevailed.

Some years ago I was seated next to a young man on an airplane, and as we traveled to our destination, we began to discuss our faith and our life circumstances. He shared with me that he and his wife had nearly given up hope of having a child of their own.

As I listened to his story, I felt God urge me to suggest to him that what he desired would indeed happen. I asked him to take my business card and please send me a note when the baby was born.

The next year I received a letter in the mail. I didn't recognize whom the letter was from, but when I opened it, inside there was a beautiful picture of a newborn baby. The young man from the airplane had sent it to me to confirm that God had indeed worked a miracle.

He said that when he got off the plane that day, he just knew something had changed. As the tears rolled down my cheeks, I thanked God for this amazing miracle and His goodness in bringing it to pass. I was so blessed by the news.

I can only imagine Sarah's friends, who must have prayed for her miracle baby for years and years, and how amazed and blessed they must have been when Isaac was at last in their midst.

Of course, the miracle exists in the One who chose to make what seemed impossible in the minds of human beings happen, and create the moment of possibility.

 May His power fill our lives even now!

A Miraculous Thought

A miracle is an event
beyond the power of
any known physical
law to produce; it is
a spiritual occurrence
produced by the
power of God,
a marvel, a wonder.

BILLY GRAHAM

When Only God Can Make a Way

THE BIBLICAL ACCOUNT

"Then Moses raised his hand over the sea, and the Lord opened up a path through the water with a strong east wind. The wind blew all that night, turning the seabed into dry land. So the people of Israel walked through the middle of the sea on dry ground, with walls of water on each side!

Then the Egyptians – all of Pharaoh's horses, chariots, and charioteers – chased them into the middle of the sea. But just before dawn the Lord looked down on the Egyptian army from the pillar of fire and cloud, and He threw their forces into total confusion. He twisted their chariot wheels, making their chariots difficult to drive. 'Let's get out of here – away from these Israelites!' the Egyptians shouted. 'The Lord is fighting for them against Egypt!'

When all the Israelites had reached the other side, the Lord said to Moses, 'Raise your hand over the sea again. Then the waters will rush back and cover the Egyptians and their chariots and charioteers.' So as the sun began to rise, Moses raised his hand over the sea, and the water rushed back into its usual place.

The Egyptians tried to escape, but the Lord swept them into the sea. Then the waters returned and covered all the chariots and charioteers – the entire army of Pharaoh. Of all the Egyptians who had chased the Israelites into the sea, not a single one survived.

But the people of Israel had walked through the middle of the sea on dry ground, as the water stood up like a wall on both sides. That is how the Lord rescued Israel from the hand of the Egyptians that day. And the Israelites saw the bodies of the Egyptians washed up on the seashore." EXODUS 14:21-30 NLT

Embracing the Miracle Moment ...

Have you ever felt trapped in a situation; surrounded on all sides by what seemed like dead ends?

Maybe you were stuck in a marriage where you had tried everything to make things work. Maybe you were trapped in a job that had no future. You may as well have been grinding bricks for your own personal Pharaoh out of bails of straw.

Then one day, things changed. You started to sense God's deliverance that somehow there would indeed be a way out and, if you stayed faithful, God would lead the way to higher ground. Many of us have had to wait for God's hand to clear a path so we could live again and become more of what He planned for us to become.

Our ancient ancestors crossed the Red Sea with fear and trembling. They knew the enemy was not far behind and that the waters of possibility would only last for so long. They had to act and act fast.

They could no longer make excuses about why life wasn't fair or why things weren't working out as they had expected. They knew what it was like to be between a rock and a hard place and they decided, with God's help, to move on.

You can too. Sometimes our circumstances can get so big and so difficult that there's no turning back; there's only the movement forward to a new hope, a promised land.

The miracle wasn't so much that the sea parted, though that was of course something out of the ordinary. The miracle was that the Israelites looked at those walls of water towering above their heads and, having no idea whether they would actually make it across or not, they took a step, then two, and picked up their belongings and their children, and moved.

God didn't mean for them to take very long. In fact, He only gave them a few short hours to accomplish the deed.

What kind of Miracle Moment do you need to help you move forward and get to the promised land God has set up for you?

What will help you believe that you can get out of the trap, the debt, the miserable job, the broken marriage and get to higher ground?

You have a Miracle Moment
coming up and you have a loving
God who is already ahead of you,
paving the way. Raise your hand
to Him and let Him help you cross over
into a new life.

One Miracle Moment

I never dreamed the day would come that I would actually get a divorce. Somehow I just imagined a small-town girl and her high-school sweetheart would find a way to make life work out for the long haul.

But through a lot of twists and turns that I never expected, I found my way to the courtroom to dissolve my marriage of thirteen years.

It was a hard day to say the least, and I was totally uncertain as to whether it was the right step to take. I was not standing on any kind of familiar ground and I hoped God would not abandon me.

At that time I was an avid reader of a little book that I still find fascinating called *God Calling*. As I turned to the reading for that particular day, it read:

"Go forward fearlessly. Do not think about the Red Sea that lies ahead. Be very sure that when you come to it the waters will part and you will pass over to your promised land of freedom."

When I got to the courtroom and saw the red-carpeted floor, and the judge called us forward to go through the narrow gate to stand at the bench, I went, strengthened by the thought that it was indeed time to pass over to the promised land of freedom.

For me, it was a Miracle Moment.

23

A Miraculous Thought

Life is a hard fight, a struggle, a wrestling with the principle of evil, hand to hand, foot to foot. Every inch of the way is disputed. The night is given to us to take breath and to pray, to drink deep at the fountain of power. The day, to use the strength which has been given to us, to go forth and to work with it till the evening.

FLORENCE NIGHTINGALE

THE BIBLICAL ACCOUNT

"Gideon said to God, 'You said You would help me save Israel. I will put some wool on the threshing floor. If there is dew only on the wool but all of the ground is dry, then I will know that You will use me to save Israel, as You said.' And that is just what happened. When Gideon got up early the next morning and squeezed the wool, he got a full bowl of water from it.

Then Gideon said to God, 'Don't be angry with me if I ask just one more thing. Please let me make one more test. Let only the wool be dry while the ground around it gets wet with dew.'

That night God did that very thing. Just the wool was dry, but the ground around it was wet with dew."

JUDGES 6:36-40 NCV

Embracing the Miracle Moment ...

Gideon's story actually starts a little earlier on when the angel of the Lord visits him as he is separating the wheat from the chaff in a winepress to keep the wheat from the Midianites.

If you remember, the Lord had given Israel over to the rule of the Midianites because Israel had refused to stop worshiping other gods.

"The angel of the Lord appeared to Gideon and said, 'The Lord is with you, mighty warrior!' Then Gideon said, 'Sir, if the Lord is with us, why are we having so much trouble? Where are the miracles our ancestors told us He did when the Lord brought them out of Egypt? But now He has left us and has handed us over to the Midianites.'

The Lord turned to Gideon and said, 'Go with your strength and save Israel from the Midianites. I am the One who is sending you.' But Gideon answered, 'Lord, how can I save Israel? My family group is the weakest in Manasseh, and I am the least important member of my family.'

The Lord answered him, 'I will be with you. It will seem as if the Midianites you are fighting are only one man.' Then Gideon said to the Lord, 'If You are pleased with me, give me proof that it is really You talking with me.'"

JUDGES 6:12-17 NCV

What's interesting is that Gideon had so many of the same insecurities we have when it comes to taking a stand for the Lord, for ourselves or for someone we love.

Notice that the angel of the Lord addressed him as "mighty warrior," yet Gideon says he's the weakest and least important member of his family.

What does it take for us to believe that our weakness brings an opportunity for God to be our strength? What does it take for us to step out in faith and realize that we are "mighty warriors" and not unimportant women in a weak family?

Even with all this conversation going pretty firmly in Gideon's direction, he still doesn't believe it. He still asks for proof that he's actually talking to the angel.

This is where our stories are also similar. This is where the human side of us must depend on the grace of God. Out of love for Gideon, and perhaps more than a little tolerance, God provides for Gideon's needs. God gives him the proof he's after – and He does it several times.

> What does it take for us to believe that our weakness brings an opportunity for God to be our strength?

Gideon's fears and his weak faith are very much in keeping with our own. He lived in a time where he witnessed his people being abused and cruelly beaten by the Midianites and he assumed that God had left the miracle business behind with his ancestors and that, perhaps, God no longer cared about them in the same way.

He assumed, doubted, and mistrusted – but he was wrong!

One Miracle Moment

At one point in my life, I put out a "Gideon fleece" so that I could try to understand the Lord's leading. It was a vulnerable time for me and it was important that I found the right kind of work to support me and my two children.

After what seemed like a nearly miraculous set of circumstances, I was interviewed for a position to be an editor at a greeting card company. I had just completed a Master's Degree in Education and thought I'd be a teacher. But then this opportunity came along and I sought the Lord's direction because it didn't fit what I assumed I was going to do with my life.

When the company called to offer me the job, I listened to the terms and conditions and told them I would consider their offer and get back to them. I then proceeded to put out my fleece. I said, "Lord, if this is Your direction for me and if I'm supposed to take this position, please do these things by the time I speak to the company again.

"Please let them know I need more time between the ending of my teaching position and starting my job with the company. Please let them know I need more money than they have offered me and please give me more vacation time to spend with my children. If these three things happen, Lord, I will trust that You are directing my steps to do this."

A few days later, I received a phone call from the company. Before asking me if I had decided whether to join them or not, they said they had some things to share with me. One thing was that they felt I might need some time between ending my teaching job and coming to work for them, so they wondered if I'd like to wait two weeks before starting the new job.

They added that they had just completed a new review of benefits and new employees would now receive two weeks of paid vacation instead of one. Finally, they said, "We can offer you $3,000 more than we first thought. Will you take the job?"

I was awed by the conversation and I know now that it was clearly God's plan for my life to take that job because much of what I do today is built on the many things I learned while I was part of that company.

God honored my fleece and gave me the answers I needed exactly as I had asked for them. It felt like a miracle to me!

God is the same yesterday, today and tomorrow. He creates miracles to help His fearfully weak children understand His grace and love and direction.

He has miracles ready and waiting for you.

A
Miraculous
Thought

When you affirm big,
believe big, and pray big,
big things happen.

NORMAN VINCENT PEALE

There's Something
Fishy about These Taxes

THE BIBLICAL ACCOUNT

"On their arrival in Capernaum, the collectors for the Temple tax came to Peter and asked him, 'Doesn't your Teacher pay the Temple tax?'

'Yes, He does,' Peter replied. Then he went into the house.

But before he had a chance to speak, Jesus asked him, 'What do you think, Peter? Do kings tax their own people or the people they have conquered?'

'They tax the people they have conquered,' Peter replied.

'Well, then,' Jesus said, 'the citizens are free! However, we don't want to offend them, so go down to the lake and throw in a line. Open the mouth of the first fish you catch, and you will find a large silver coin. Take it and pay the tax for both of us.'" MATTHEW 17:24-27 NLT

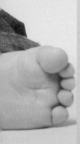

Embracing the Miracle Moment ...

Jesus and His followers lived much like we live today. They worked, they paid taxes, and they did their best to make it through the day.

The Temple tax was one of the local obligations. It was paid to help with the upkeep of the Temple and required the equivalent of two day's wages from those who paid it. It's interesting that when Peter was approached by the tax collector and had to answer the question of whether or not Jesus paid the Temple tax, Peter defended his Master and simply responded as though Jesus would naturally pay the tax. He did that even though he wasn't really sure he was right.

Peter went to discuss the Temple tax issue with Jesus, probably wondering if they would pay the tax since they had not done so up to that point, but Jesus already knew what he was going to say. Yes, it's possible that Jesus saw him talking to the tax collector, but perhaps Jesus just knew what was on Peter's mind.

The question of who really should pay the tax reflects Jesus' understanding that the Temple actually belonged to Him, as the Son of the King of the universe, and that His followers would belong to Him and therefore not have to pay the tax.

As the children of the King, Jesus is saying that they don't actually have to pay the tax, but then He creates a way for them to do so because He realizes that the tax collectors might not see things the same way.

The miracle, and the fun part of this concern for Peter, is that Jesus offered him a way to solve the problem that was both clever and probably instantly bonding between the two friends. Peter was a fisherman, after all, so casting a line into the waters to find a fish with a coin in its mouth, was a delightful solution.

Perhaps if someone like me had been having this conversation with Jesus He would have said,

"Go to the bookstore and pick up the first book you see about blessings and you'll find a check in the back corner sleeve."

I could relate to that environment, and finding the check in the book would simply be more evidence of God's love for me at work.

One Miracle Moment

Money issues plague all of us at times, and wondering where we'll get what we need to pay the taxes, or some other bill, is not always easy. Sometimes God does the clever and surprising and amazing for us, too, like He did for Peter in the previous story.

One such story stems from my own family before I was born, with my dad, mom and eldest two siblings. When my father returned from Japan after the Second World War, he worked at whatever jobs he could find to support his young wife and two babies.

Since jobs weren't easily available, he found himself without work for a time and they had to make do with whatever little income he still received from the government. At one point they were no longer able to pay the bill on their old truck and after a few months, the bill was $300. That was a lot of money for them and there was no way to pay it.

One day a collection's agent came to visit with the intention of repossessing the only means of transportation.

When the agent came to the door, my mother greeted him with a baby on her hip, a smile on her face, and offered him a cup of coffee. The man came in and noticed the plastic on the windows to help keep out the cold, the iron my mother was heating on the stove to do her ironing, and another baby in a high chair.

He was amazed at how much my mother was trying to take care of things. When my dad came in a few minutes later, the man addressed him and said that he could see they had fallen on hard times. Dad told him they were doing the best they could and he hoped to get more work at a local creamery soon, but of course, without a vehicle, that would be even more difficult.

My dad says he doesn't really know what happened next except that the man left and never said a word about taking the truck.

In fact, he discovered later that the bill had been paid. He and my mom were grateful for the miracle. For all my dad and mom had to work with, it might just as well have come from the fish's mouth.

A Miraculous Thought

Be on the lookout for mercies.
The more we look for them,
the more of them we will see ...
Better to lose count while
naming your blessings
than to lose your blessings
to counting your troubles.

MALTIE D. BABCOCK

43

THE BIBLICAL ACCOUNT

"Jesus got into a boat, and His followers went with Him. A great storm arose on the lake so that waves covered the boat, but Jesus was sleeping. His followers went to Him and woke Him, saying, 'Lord, save us! We will drown!'

Jesus answered,

'Why are you afraid?'

You don't have enough faith.' Then Jesus got up and gave a command to the wind and the waves, and it became completely calm.

The men were amazed and said, 'What kind of man is this? Even the wind and the waves obey Him!'"

MATTHEW 8:23-27 NCV

Embracing the Miracle Moment ...

Facing the sudden storms of life is not easy for any of us. Things can change in an instant.

The smooth flight through the skies becomes a turbulent one; the waves come crashing onto the shoreline where we were sunning just moments before; or we're abruptly faced with loss or health issues or some kind of drama that we didn't anticipate. Those changes can be frightening.

This story of Jesus and His followers in a boat off the eastern shore of the Sea of Galilee, near the village of Khersa, demonstrates a very real aspect of what faith calls us to do.

We can imagine the frightened followers – some of them seafaring fisherman, the others inexperienced in the complexities of winds and waves – and their reactions as the water began to come up over the edge of the boat, bouncing them around, threatening their very existence.

Then imagine their Leader, seemingly unconcerned, catching a little shuteye, sleeping like a baby in a rocking cradle. Somehow Jesus doesn't even seem aware of their impending peril. Why is that?

Recently, I was floating down a river between Panama and Costa Rica in a dugout canoe. I was so overwhelmed by the incredible beauty around me and the diversity of the plant life that I didn't actually pay attention when the boat hit a rapid and a rough spot in the river that carried us along.

As the two guides worked to take care of the situation, I found myself totally unconcerned, unable to move

45

my thinking past the awesome Creator who had brought me to that place.

As we moved along further into the jungle, my host tapped me on the shoulder. He remarked how impressed he was that I had managed to concentrate on the beauty of the surroundings as we entered the rapids. He said, "You were so focused on what was beautiful, you hardly noticed the difficulty we were in."

Since it was my first time visiting the rainforest reserve, I had a lot of preconceived ideas of what might be scary, from the thought of alligators in the river to spiders and bats. The truth is none of those things caused me a moment of stress the whole time I was there.

I was so certain it was God's plan for me to be there that nothing could shake my confidence in that, and so I remained at peace.

Perhaps Jesus had some sense of that same kind of peace as He lay in the boat with His followers. Perhaps He was so focused on the idea that He was doing exactly what God wanted Him to do that certainly some winds and waves could do nothing to stop the plan.

His faith rested, and so did He, in the hands of His Father.

How nice for us when we can put our faith in that same boat!

One Miracle Moment

I have a friend who was second in command on a Navy warship during the Gulf War. He told me that at one point the men were pretty nervous as they ventured into known enemy territory, especially since a ship just like theirs had suffered great losses just days before.

Since it was important for the men to stay as calm as possible, he decided to set an example for them. He set up a deck chair in the middle of the ship and, as they were passing through the thick of enemy waters, he sat in the chair and took a nap.

He said his tactic made quite an impression on his men. They figured that if he was so confident about their safety that he could sleep on the deck, then they should share his faith and believe everything would be okay.

As it turned out, staying calm paid off for the whole group and they got through those waters safely.

Maybe my friend took note of the way Jesus slept during the stormy seas. Maybe sleeping through the midst of the storm kept the waters calm and the waves at peace in a miraculous way.

Sometimes God creates the miracle. Sometimes He puts us in charge of being the miracle.

Staying calm in the stormy seas requires faith either way.

A
Miraculous
Thought

We live by faith, not by sight.

2 CORINTHIANS 5:7 NIV

The person of faith may face
death as Columbus faced his first
voyage from the shores of Spain.
What lies beyond the sea he cannot
tell; all his special expectation may
be mistaken, but his insight into the
clear meaning of present facts may
persuade him beyond the doubt
that the sea has another shore.

HARRY EMERSON FOSDICK

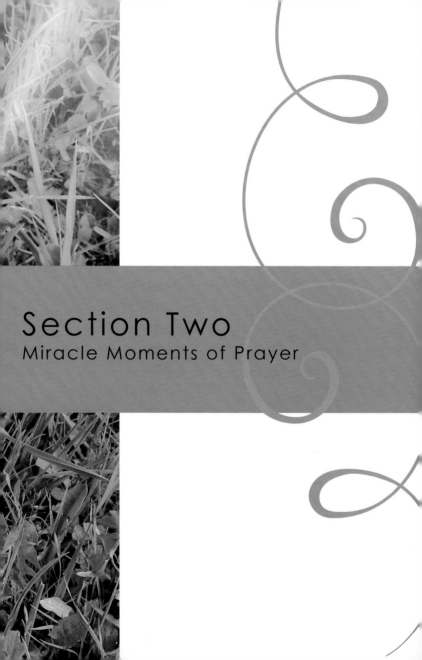

Section Two
Miracle Moments of Prayer

As women of God, we tend to be women of prayer. For us, all things great or small need to be placed in God's care. Whatever forms we adopt for prayer, we appreciate knowing there's a listening ear, a guiding hand, a loving God who hears what we have to say.

In a world where listening to each other, much less listening to God, is almost unusual, it's a miraculous practice all by itself.

As Matthew reminded us, our spirits may well be willing, but our bodies are sometimes too tired to begin. When we do make prayer a natural part of our lives, though, we begin to build the kind of relationship that helps us gain insight and receive answers.

Little by little, we see God's hand and His very intentional answers coming our way – sometimes before we even ask. We discover that prayer is truly effective, even causing miracles in our own lives or in the lives of others in our prayer chain. Jesus even went so far as to say,

> "Whatever you ask for in My name, that I will do, that the Father may be glorified in the Son. If you ask anything in My name, I will do it."
> JOHN 14:13-14 NKJV

When was the last time you got an offer like that? That's an invitation to say yes to! It's a blank check from your lips to God's ear. That is a pretty practical incentive to pray … without ceasing.

Colossians 4:2 encourages us to "devote ourselves to prayer, being watchful and thankful."

If the Bible takes prayer so seriously, we have every reason to do so too. After all, as somebody once said, "The best way to get on your feet is to first get on your knees."

The miracles recorded in the following pages come from the prayers of women and men who kept a constant connection to God's ear, sometimes fainting, but always returning to the task until answers came.

One Miracle Moment

A friend of mine told me a delightful story of a Miracle Moment in her life. At the time she lived near Scottsdale, Arizona, and when she went for treatments at the cancer center there, she would often stop at a small Hispanic chapel nearby to pray and pour her heart out to God.

She and her mother sometimes met at this chapel to comfort each other, offer encouragement, and pray. Since this chapel was a good forty minutes or so from either of their homes they actually visited there anonymously, not as part of the congregation, as neither of them spoke Spanish.

One particular day, as my friend left the treatment center after a rather discouraging consultation with her doctor, she found her way to the chapel – not even realizing in what direction she was driving. She had just planned on going home, but somehow in her state of sadness and tears, she had turned into the road that led to the chapel.

Noticing that the lot was full, she assumed some special service must be going on and was planning to just drive by when a very distinct voice told her to "drive in and find a parking space."

Not fully aware of why, she did as she was directed and discovered the only space left was right in front by the door. She parked and got out.

Standing in the back of the main room, she discovered the church was packed. Crying behind her sunglasses, she eventually noticed a man waving at her, inviting her to join him in the pew. He had already made room for her. She thought it was a bit strange since she didn't know him and many others were also standing, but she settled in beside him, offered a weary smile, and began to pray.

Since the service was all in Spanish, she kept her head down, crying softly and not paying full attention to the Mass she couldn't really understand. She just hoped for some sense of peace.

Then a miracle happened. She heard the priest, who was in the midst of prayers, speak her full Christian name in English. It was such a surprise to her that she looked up, startled. Awed, she realized how amazing it was that she was even seated in the church for that particular service.

Though her mother may have put her name in the prayer intentions box at some time, it still seemed like a miracle to my friend that she was actually there at that precise moment to hear a crystal clear calling of her name in that little church.

She felt like God was letting her know that He was still in charge and that she could leave all the details of the things that frightened her up to Him.

He had orchestrated a way for her to get the message that He was indeed paying attention. It was a Miracle Moment for my friend and she left the church with a smile on her face.

Embracing the Miracle Moment ...

Even though we may be tempted to think that miracles are always about the extraordinary; those unexplainable things that go beyond the limits of physical science or our general intelligence, we can sometimes see the miracles that arise from the ordinary.

Certainly visiting the church wasn't so extraordinary for my friend, who often stopped by there after her treatments, but the visit that day was orchestrated and divinely intended.

Had she chosen to believe that God did not hear her concerns about breast cancer, or that she couldn't get much out of a service in a language she couldn't understand, then she might not have listened to the voice bidding her to stop and park.

Perhaps if the kind man had not invited her to sit down, she would have given up and left without hearing the priest mention her name during the prayer.

Sometimes, we have to embrace the small things. We have to believe that the familiar surroundings can come to life with **new hope and direction**. We have to keep walking in the faith that we've been called to follow.

A Miraculous Thought

A miracle is a supernatural event, whose antecedent forces are beyond our finite vision, whose design is the display of almighty power for the accomplishment of almighty purposes, and whose immediate result, as regards man, is his recognition of God as the Supreme Ruler of all things, and of His will as the only supreme law.

ABBOTT E. KITTREDGE

The Wedding at Cana

"In that place there were six stone water jars that the Jews used in their washing ceremony. Each jar held about twenty or thirty gallons. Jesus said to the servants, 'Fill the jars with water.' So they filled the jars to the top. Then He said to them, 'Now take some out and give it to the master of the feast.' So they took the water to the master. When he tasted it, the water had become wine.

He did not know where the wine came from, but the servants who had brought the water knew. The master of the wedding called the bridegroom and said to him, 'People always serve the best wine first. Later, after the guests have been drinking awhile, they serve the cheaper wine. But you have saved the best wine till now.'

So in Cana of Galilee Jesus did His first miracle. There He showed His glory, and His followers believed in Him."
JOHN 2:6-11 NCV

Jesus takes the ordinary and makes it extraordinary.

Sometimes He does so by calling your name out loud, sometimes by turning water into wine, changing the direction of your life, or creating a new space where none existed previously.

Embrace the One who loves you and receive His miracles designed just for you.

Another Miracle Moment
of Prayer

Albert Einstein once said we can live our lives as though nothing is a miracle or as though everything is a miracle.

If you pause long enough to think about it, you are probably hard-pressed to imagine that "nothing is a miracle." It seems that most of us are privy to one miracle or another.

What we choose to believe about it or how we choose to share it with others is another matter. One of my own miracles happened rather recently.

I had moved lock, stock, and barrel to a new city, where I had neither family nor friends, and did so on the faith that this was the next step my life needed to take.

Though I hadn't been fully engaged in my former job, I wasn't so sure about leaving my parents or my sisters who lived close by. But the new job was based on creating Christian materials and I believed there couldn't be a better calling than that.

Almost from the first day the new job was a challenge, but I tried to have a positive attitude and roll with the punches. And there were many!

Almost every week new ways of doing business were ushered in, while I was still immersed in learning the previous ones. It also turned out that three of the members of my staff left the company for one reason or another and none of them were replaced.

In addition to that, I took on the management of the department's biggest project, which was both exhausting and exhilarating as we moved through the process. Needless to say, it was more than a learning curve. It was more like a learning obstacle course.

After about a year, I started gaining confidence and a better sense of my work and was being groomed to become Vice President of my department. I felt good about the promotion because I was really going to do more of what I do best, which involves creative product development. When the promotion date came, however, I was told that I had to wait for the budget to be approved before it became official and that we would have the word about two weeks later.

Two weeks later, I was laid off and the people who worked for me were either laid off too, or moved to other areas. So, everything was ripped apart and I wondered why God had moved me there and what He was doing. I hoped it was not just so I could feel like an idiot.

If you've ever been laid off you know that no matter how they try to couch it, no matter how well you feel you were doing, you end up feeling as though you've been kicked in the stomach

A couple of months after the lay-off, I decided to attend the industry trade show in Florida because I thought it would be a good opportunity for me to network and let people know I was available again. As my flight landed in Orlando, I prayed that God would grant me divine appointments and that this show would be His opportunity to help me get back on my feet.

It was a good show and I felt my spirits rise as I met with old friends and acquaintances. I received positive feedback and some potential opportunities.

However, at one point as I was simply "walking" the show to get an overview, I stopped at a small greeting card company's booth to see what they had to offer. Since I come from the greeting card industry and there are just a few strong players in the Christian market, I felt led to stop by.

It was indeed a divine appointment. As I sat and listened to the needs that this company had to grow and become more, I knew I was one of the right people to help make that happen. The miracle was for me as much as it was for the company. We both had a need to be creating and becoming more than what we were.

We knew we were meant to be furthering God's work in very real ways. When I was invited to work with the team, I accepted the offer. There was no other choice since God had set everything up for that purpose.

Later, as I discussed things with my new friend, the

original creator of this company and its president, he told me his story. He said that he had prayed to God and said to Him that he always did what he could to help others.

He gave from his heart and he offered his best. Then he asked God, "How come there is never anyone to help me?"

He told me that when I came along that day, just stopping at his booth to see how he was doing, he knew I was God's answer. Wow!

The beauty of this is that it means any of us can be a miracle for someone at any time. Any of us can be God's answer for someone else. **All we need to do is be open to His leading and be ready to answer.**

That was the miracle that came as an answer to prayers because we asked God to lead, and He did.

Embracing the Miracle Moment ...

In a recent visit to a client of mine in Costa Rica, my friend and I explored an active volcano. When we first arrived we could see the volcano in all its splendor in every detail. The textures and the colors were magnificent. It was like seeing God's creative hand at work and breathing in the mists of adventure.

However, within an hour of our arrival, the clouds moved in and we couldn't see the volcano any more at all – even though we were standing at the very edge of it. We decided to walk along the black sand perimeter while we still could. My friend called out to me to look at a tree on the opposite side of the flat sand crater where we were.

When I spotted the tree, he asked me to close my eyes and listen to his voice and walk toward it. I smiled at the idea and, noting that the ground didn't seem especially hazardous, I closed my eyes, listened, and walked. After a while though, I couldn't hear his voice and I stopped walking. I called out to him and he spoke again, suggesting I go another fifty steps or so.

I did, but without his voice to guide me. At the designated spot, I called to him again and opened my eyes. The tree that I thought I was heading for directly was now about ninety degrees off to my left. I was amazed because I was so sure I was going in exactly the right direction.

Isn't that how it is for us with God? When we are really listening to His voice we can walk on the path He designed for us with a certain sense of ease. When we stop listening, even when we think we're doing what He might want, we tend to go off on our own and, before we know it, we're not even on the path anymore. We may not have even realized that we walked away from Him, but somehow we did.

As I looked at the tree I thought I was heading for and realized how far I was from the mark, I began to wonder what I needed to do to be a better listener. How could I stay more clearly on the path?

When we look at our lives, it's fairly easy to see what happens if we don't listen to God's voice. Maybe we are meant to be the answer to someone else's prayer and yet we walk by totally unaware of the opportunity. I tend to believe that if God designs it though, He'll help us discover the plan, so it could be a momentary fear, but it isn't reality.

The truth is that God will find a way to present the miracle opportunity to you over and over. He isn't trying to play a game with your heart and mind. He wants you to succeed and He wants you to be a part of the work He needs to have accomplished.

The challenge is to keep our hearts open to the possibilities and to seek them willingly and lovingly. The miracle is already there, waiting to happen.

A Miraculous Thought

A miracle is an event which creates faith. That is the purpose and nature of miracles. Frauds deceive. An event which creates faith does not deceive: therefore it is not a fraud, but a miracle.

GEORGE BERNARD SHAW

Miracle Moments Are Everywhere

"So we must listen very carefully to the truth we have heard, or we may drift away from it. For the message God delivered through angels has always stood firm, and every violation of the law and every act of disobedience was punished. So what makes us think we can escape if we ignore this great salvation that was first announced by the Lord Jesus Himself and then delivered to us by those who heard Him speak? And God confirmed the message by giving signs and wonders and various miracles and gifts of the Holy Spirit whenever He chose."

HEBREWS 2:1-4 NLT

We've spent time reviewing some of the biblical miracles and our response to them. We've seen some present-day examples to show us that God is the same yesterday, today, and forever!

He still walks with us, talks with us when we're ready to listen, and provides miraculous evidence of just how real and how close He is to our everyday lives.

From here, we'll look at a sampling of His great deeds in the lives of ordinary people; the same kind of people He sacrificed Himself for centuries ago.

Let's look at the work of the Holy Spirit in these brief stories, because this Spirit is working in our lives at this very moment!

A Story from 36,000 Feet Above the Ground

It just so happened (of course, I say that with a smile, because nothing just happens when you're walking with God) that I sat next to a woman on an airplane who was attending the same Christian conference I was attending.

She told me that she wasn't sure why she was going because she was discouraged about God and didn't know if He even heard her prayers anymore.

She had prayed for years for her brother's salvation and he now had lung cancer, so her fears were getting the best of her. She also prayed for her father who was in a nursing home.

As we talked, we discussed how hard it is sometimes to believe in miracles or even the hope that God is ready to do something to ease the situation at hand. I encouraged the woman to simply remain open

to possibility, to let God sit with her and walk with her at the conference, renewing and strengthening her, and then pray more to see just what He would do. I offered to pray with her as well.

A few weeks later she sent me a note and told me a miracle story. She had spoken to me on the plane about her brother with lung cancer who did not have long to live and who appeared to have no personal relationship with God. Her sorrow was two-fold in losing him.

However, God chose to initiate a personal relationship with her brother, honoring her prayers in this way. After chemo treatments and radiation, the doctors determined that all the cancer was gone and that no further treatment was needed. To the doctors' surprise, her brother was healed.

The healing is the beginning of the miracle. The willingness to accept divine intervention because of the prayers of many on his behalf now remains with this woman's brother. He has experienced a miraculous recovery, a gift from God to give him more time to grow and live in His grace. For everyone who prays for others, for both physical and spiritual healing, comes genuine rejoicing.

This woman's prayers and those of her friends made a difference. It's a miracle created from love. In this case, God demonstrates again that His love is so great that He acts on behalf of those in need – sometimes before they even know Him personally. Isn't that the gift of Jesus for all of us?

When we trust
God's promises,
He never fails us.

Pennies from Heaven

Ever since I was a child, I have enjoyed the idea that if I found a penny on the sidewalk or the pavement, or wherever I happened to be walking, it would mean that an angel had been there just before me and knew I was coming.

Over the years, I often smile when I see those pennies because it seems to happen just when I need a gentle reminder that I'm not here all alone and that God is always with me. I like knowing that I'm not alone, that God is very aware of my presence no matter where I am.

These penny reminders strike me as little miracles because they appear when I least expect them, and yet have a spiritual need for them.

At one point, as I struggled with having the financial means to keep paying my bills and planning for a future, I had a different kind of "penny" experience. I was walking on a quiet street in Colorado Springs, praying my way along, trying to understand why having enough money always seemed like such an issue for me.

Knowing that security was one of my main conscious needs, I wondered why it was the one thing I never seemed to actually have – at least not in the monetary sense.

As I wound my way around the roadside, I saw something shining in the sunlight and walked over to see what it was. Sure enough it was a quarter. Even though I had stopped picking up pennies when I found them – thinking others might need the same reminder I received –

I picked up this quarter and put it in my pocket. I thanked God for the reminder of twenty-five angels walking on before me, laughed to myself and went on. As I continued to think about my financial difficulty, I asked God why it was so hard to believe that He would provide for me.

Walking a little further, I spotted another shiny object on the road. It turned out to be another quarter. When I picked it up, I felt God ask me if it was hard for me to believe that He could provide for me just that easily. In other words, He could pave the way with quarters; I just had to believe He would do so.

With that message, and the idea that perhaps now fifty angels had walked ahead of me on the path that day, I determined to take God at His word. I changed my thinking. Ever since, I have believed in God's provision and I have never found myself in quite that same kind of financial dismay.

> The miracle for me is that believing is receiving. As long as I believe in God's provision, the miracle continues.

Like the boy with five loaves and two fish, I can believe that whatever I have, it will always be more than what I need.

Every good thing comes from heaven above, and the One who provides for my spirit, provides for my every need as well. When we trust His promises, He never fails us.

Defining Miracle Moments

A Miracle Moment is one that causes you to pause and reflect in a new way on what happened to change your thinking, your direction, or your opportunity to understand more fully the love God has for you.

They seem to burst forth in the desert of your circumstance like wildflowers on the hillside. One moment everything is cold and barren, and the next moment it teems with life again.

Those are miraculous events and we each experience them as gifts beyond measure. Sometimes they are moments that have been the subject of unending prayers, answered in awe.

Other times they are simply the light pouring through the windows of our hearts at just the right moment.

A Miraculous Thought

A gentle word,
a kind look,
a good-natured smile
can work wonders
and accomplish
miracles.

WILLIAM HAZLITT

Miracle Moments Are All Around Us

We all know stories that take our breath away and make us pause in sheer joy and wonder to realize what God has done in a particular moment, in some special way to come to the aid of His children. Let's finish our look at Miracle Moments by doing just that, stopping long enough to take in a truth, an instance, an unexplained happening in the lives of those around us. Here are a few just for you:

Traveling on a freeway in the fast lane, mud splattered across my windshield only to be made worse by running the wiper blades. With no washer fluid available and nearly blind to the traffic ahead, I prayed for rain. It rained. It rained on my window only.

A thirteen-year-old girl and her eighteen-year-old boyfriend get in trouble. They stay together and get married. They have four children. They are still married after sixty-three years. The miracle is love.

A husband and wife have a fight. The wife is feeling sad and wonders if God sees her or loves her. She takes a walk to think things through. Spotting something shiny on the ground, she picks it up and sees that it's a little medallion. It says, "God loves you." She smiles at God's grace.

A woman takes her beloved pet to a vet for treatment. She feels uneasy about the medication and prays for guidance about whether she should use it or not. She finds a piece of paper, long since forgotten, sticking out of her notebook with the number of another vet. She calls and the dog is put on another type of medication. The first one would have been fatal to her pet.

A young man works hard to create a company that serves God and people. He doesn't often get past his workload to learn of the impact his work has on others. A woman stops to tell him that she received one of his products and it changed her life. She had been without hope and was feeling suicidal. Then she received one of his cards from a friend and it gave her a sense of hope and a reason to live.

A woman believes that God shows His love for her by putting hummingbirds in her life. After being diagnosed with cancer, she finds herself walking down a beach and before she knows it four hummingbirds have surrounded her. She believes God's message of protection. She beats the cancer.

A young couple with two children is out of work and can't pay their bills. A collector comes to take away their only vehicle. On seeing the plastic on the windows to keep out the cold, a small stove to keep the babies warm, and the effort the couple is making to stay alive, the collector leaves. The $300 bill is mysteriously paid in full and the young man finds a new job.

A woman is fired from her job and doesn't understand why because she worked really hard. She prays for guidance, and reads a parable in the Bible where she gets an idea for a job opportunity. The job comes the very day her severance runs out and provides a whole new opportunity for her to achieve skills needed for her life's work. She sees the grace of God at work.

A disturbed father threatens to kidnap his children from their mother even though he has no means to care for them. Even with the police on the look out, he manages to get to the children and put them in his old van. Just as he is trying to escape, the mother returns from the neighbors and sees him pulling out of the driveway. Suddenly the van door falls off the car. The father is forced to stop and the children are safe.

A woman driving down a highway sees a suspicious in- cident – a man picking up two young boys. Alerted by the Holy Spirit that the situation is bad, the woman turns around and drives back. She yells at the man to leave the boys alone and he drives off without them. She picks up the boys and takes them safely to the police station.

The Miracle of Women

There are countless miracle stories. You can search the Web for them or you can search your heart and life experience to find them. You know they happen because you are sensitive to the prompting of the Holy Spirit in your life.

Perhaps God graced women with a special sensitivity to desire more of Him and to see more of Him in each daily step. Perhaps He just knew we would need the benefit of His love and His hand as we take on the challenges that confront us day to day.

Whatever the reason, we can know more of Him because He desires to show us that He is present in all that we do.

Miracle Moments are gifts of love to keep us connected, walking closer to Him wherever life takes us. We can go forward then without fear, without worry, and without excuses, knowing we're loved and watched over by the Savior of the world, the God of mercy and hope who gives us breath and life every day.

You are His miracle in the world. You share more moments that change the lives of those around you than any evangelist will ever do.

You are His arms, His heart, and His compassion in the world. You are His choice to give and to receive Miracle Moments.

A Miraculous Thought

All things are possible to the one who believes; still more
to the one who hopes; still more to the one who loves,
and most of all to the one who practices all three.

BROTHER LAWRENCE